תְּפִלַּת שַׁחֲרִית לְשַׁבָּת

THE SHABBAT MORNING SERVICE

BOOK 3

The
Torah Service
& Selected Additional Prayers

סֵדֶר קְרִאַת הַתּוֹרָה

תְּפִלַּת שַׁחֲרִית לְשַׁבָּת

THE SHABBAT MORNING SERVICE

3 The Torah Service & Selected Additional Prayers

סֵדֶר קְרִאַת הַתּוֹרָה

Commentary by Jules Harlow

Exercises by Roberta Osser Baum

BEHRMAN HOUSE

Designer Robert J. O'Dell

Illustrator Nachman Levine

Project Editor Ruby G. Strauss

ISBN: 0-87441-449-0

Manufactured in the United States of America

INTRODUCTION

Every Shabbat and Festival Service includes a reading from the Torah. The Torah is the first five books of the Bible (Genesis, Exodus, Leviticus, Numbers and Deuteronomy). The entire Torah is read in each year's cycle of Shabbat services. It is divided into sections known as *parashiyot* (singular: *parashah*). Each Shabbat is assigned a specific *parashah*, by which it is often called (for example: Shabbat *B'reishith*). Some congregations follow the custom of reading one-third of a section each Shabbat, thus finishing the entire Torah once every three years. This practice is known as the triennial cycle. The Torah is also read on Monday and Thursday mornings and on Shabbat afternoon.

Before and after the Torah Reading, elaborate rituals are performed and various passages recited. These emphasize the importance of the Torah in our tradition. They help each of us to express our love and respect for the Torah and its teachings.

In the second book in this series, you studied the Amidah for Shabbat morning. Another Amidah is recited after the Torah Service is completed. It is called *Musaf*, an additional Amidah, because of the additional rituals followed on Shabbat in ancient times. The *Musaf* Amidah is not included in this book. It differs from the Morning *(Shaharit)* Amidah in its middle (fourth) *berakhah*.

This book contains the passages which conclude the Shabbat (and the Festival) Service. Most of this last section is poetry. It is usually sung by the congregation. Singing together creates a bond among members of each congregation, just as the words of the Torah create a bond between the members of all congregations everywhere – past, present and future.

The Torah Reading is an essential feature of the synagogue service on Shabbat. The synagogue is not only a house of worship but also a house of study and instruction. When we read and study Torah, as when we pray, we take our place in the chain of tradition which binds our people together. These passages are recited before the Torah is read. (Lines 1,2 and 5 are verses from the Book of Psalms.)

סֵדֶר הוֹצָאַת סֵפֶר הַתּוֹרָה

אֵין כָּמוֹךְ begins the Torah Service. It is chanted before the Ark is opened. In this passage, we praise our eternal God, and we ask God to bless His people with strength and with peace. We also pray for the welfare of Zion and Jerusalem.

1 אֵין כָּמוֹךְ בָאֱלֹהִים אֲדֹנָי, וְאֵין כְּמַעֲשֶׂיךָ.

2 מַלְכוּתְךָ מַלְכוּת כָּל־עֹלָמִים, וּמֶמְשַׁלְתְּךָ בְּכָל־

3 דֹר וָדֹר.

4 יְיָ מֶלֶךְ, יְיָ מָלָךְ, יְיָ יִמְלֹךְ לְעֹלָם וָעֶד.

5 יְיָ עֹז לְעַמּוֹ יִתֵּן, יְיָ יְבָרֵךְ אֶת־עַמּוֹ בַשָּׁלוֹם.

6 אַב הָרַחֲמִים, הֵיטִיבָה בִרְצוֹנְךָ אֶת־צִיּוֹן, תִּבְנֶה

7 חוֹמוֹת יְרוּשָׁלָיִם. כִּי בְךָ לְבַד בָּטָחְנוּ, מֶלֶךְ אֵל

8 רָם וְנִשָּׂא, אֲדוֹן עוֹלָמִים.

The Ark is opened and the following passages are sung. These words of prayer recall the association of the Torah, God's gift, with Moses and with Jerusalem and Zion.

9 וַיְהִי בִּנְסֹעַ הָאָרֹן וַיֹּאמֶר מֹשֶׁה:

10 קוּמָה יְיָ וְיָפֻצוּ אֹיְבֶיךָ, וְיָנֻסוּ מְשַׂנְאֶיךָ מִפָּנֶיךָ.

11 כִּי מִצִּיּוֹן תֵּצֵא תוֹרָה, וּדְבַר יְיָ מִירוּשָׁלָיִם.

12 בָּרוּךְ שֶׁנָּתַן תּוֹרָה לְעַמּוֹ יִשְׂרָאֵל בִּקְדֻשָּׁתוֹ.

Blessed be He who, in His holiness, gave the Torah to His people Israel.

After the Torah is taken from the Ark, these lines are sung.

13 שְׁמַע יִשְׂרָאֵל יְיָ אֱלֹהֵינוּ יְיָ אֶחָד.

Hear O Israel: the Lord our God, the Lord is One.

14 אֶחָד אֱלֹהֵינוּ, גָּדוֹל אֲדוֹנֵינוּ, קָדוֹשׁ שְׁמוֹ.

One is our God; great is our Lord; holy is His name.

15 גַּדְּלוּ לַייָ אִתִּי וּנְרוֹמְמָה שְׁמוֹ יַחְדָּו.

Extol the Lord with me, and together let us exalt His name.

As the Torah is carried in a procession, the reader and the congregation sing this passage, It praises God's greatness and power as Ruler of the World, and acclaims God's holiness.

16 לְךָ יְיָ הַגְּדֻלָּה וְהַגְּבוּרָה וְהַתִּפְאֶרֶת וְהַנֵּצַח

17 וְהַהוֹד.

18 כִּי כֹל בַּשָּׁמַיִם וּבָאָרֶץ, לְךָ יְיָ הַמַּמְלָכָה

19 וְהַמִּתְנַשֵּׂא לְכֹל לְרֹאשׁ.

20 רוֹמְמוּ יְיָ אֱלֹהֵינוּ וְהִשְׁתַּחֲווּ לַהֲדֹם רַגְלָיו, קָדוֹשׁ

21 הוּא.

22 רוֹמְמוּ יְיָ אֱלֹהֵינוּ וְהִשְׁתַּחֲווּ לְהַר קָדְשׁוֹ, כִּי קָדוֹשׁ

23 יְיָ אֱלֹהֵינוּ.

9

סֵדֶר הוֹצָאַת סֵפֶר הַתּוֹרָה

PRAYER STUDY

These words are very significant for our people:

יִשְׂרָאֵל   צִיּוֹן   תּוֹרָה   יְרוּשָׁלַיִם   מֹשֶׁה

Israel   Zion   Torah   Jerusalem   Moses

Complete each word.

Then write the English meaning below each.

יִשְׂרָאֵל   צִיּוֹן   תּוֹרָה   יְרוּשָׁלַיִם   מֹשֶׁה

Find and lightly circle each word (lines 6,7,9,11,12,13).

Complete the words in each phrase.

6 הֵיטִיבָה בִרְצוֹנְךָ אֶת צִיּוֹן

6-7 תִּבְנֶה חוֹמוֹת יְרוּשָׁלָיִם

9 וַיְהִי בִּנְסֹעַ הָאָרֹן וַיֹּאמֶר מֹשֶׁה

11 כִּי מִצִּיּוֹן תֵּצֵא תוֹרָה

11 וּדְבַר יי מִירוּשָׁלָיִם

12 בָּרוּךְ שֶׁנָּתַן תּוֹרָה

12 לְעַמּוֹ יִשְׂרָאֵל בִּקְדֻשָּׁתוֹ

13 שְׁמַע יִשְׂרָאֵל יי אֱלֹהֵינוּ יי אֶחָד

=== **READING CHALLENGE** ===

Can you read each phrase without a mistake?

סֵדֶר הוֹצָאַת סֵפֶר הַתּוֹרָה

These words are found in lines 1-8.

line 1

אֵין כָּמֹוךָ	וְאֵין כְּמַעֲשֶׂיךָ
there is none like You	and there are no deeds like Yours

line 2

מַלְכוּתֶךָ	וּמֶמְשַׁלְתְּךָ	מַלְכוּת
Your kingdom	and Your rule	kingdom

line 4

יְיָ מָלָךְ	יְיָ מֶלֶךְ	יְיָ יִמְלֹךְ
the Lord was king	the Lord is king	the Lord will be king

line 5

עַמּוֹ	יְיָ	בַשָּׁלוֹם	יְבָרֵךְ
His people	Lord	with peace	bless

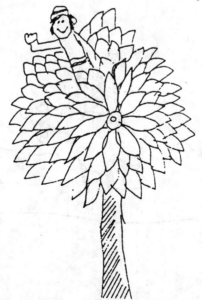

line 6

הֵיטְבָה	הָרַחֲמִים	בִּרְצוֹנְךָ	צִיּוֹן
show goodness	compassion	with Your will	Zion

lines 6-7

יְרוּשָׁלַיִם	חוֹמוֹת	תִּבְנֶה
Jerusalem	walls	build

lines 7-8

אֲדוֹן עוֹלָמִים	בָּטָחְנוּ	רָם וְנִשָּׂא
Eternal Lord	we trust	high and exalted

READING CHALLENGE:

Can you read each Key Word and Phrase without a mistake?

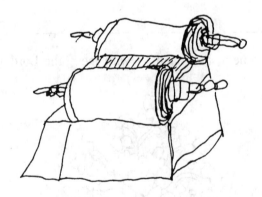

These words are found in lines 13-15

יִשְׂרָאֵל	אֲדוֹנֵינוּ	אֱלֹהֵינוּ	שְׁמַע
Israel	our Lord (Master)	our God	hear

אִתִּי	אֶחָד	וּנְרוֹמְמָה	גָּדוֹל	לַיְיָ
with me	one	and exalt	great	to the Lord

יַחְדָּו	גַּדְּלוּ	שְׁמוֹ	קָדוֹשׁ	יְיָ
together	extol	His name	holy	Lord

Write each Hebrew sentence. Begin on the right!

_____ _____ _____ _____ _____ _____

| One | Lord | our God | Lord | Israel | Hear |

_____ _____ _____ _____ _____ _____

| His name | holy | our Lord | great | our God | One |

_____ _____ _____ _____ _____ _____

| together | His name | and exalt | with me | the Lord | Extol |

God's name is written in different ways.

יְיָ   יְהֹוָה   אֲדֹנָי   —————————

אֵל   אֱלֹהִים

Write the three names of God which are pronounced exactly the same.

—————————   —————————   —————————

Read each name aloud.

How is "Adonai" spelled in line 1? _____

How is "Adonai" spelled in line 4? _____

Find God's name יְיָ in lines 1-23.

Lightly circle יְיָ each time you find it.

In line 8 God's name is written אֲדוֹן.

אֲדוֹן means "Master of" or "Lord of."

אֲדוֹן עוֹלָמִים means "Eternal Lord."

Find and lightly circle the phrase in line 8.

Write the phrase here. _____

Add אדון to the list above.

God's name אדוֹן is written very much like His name

_____, "My Lord".

15

Write God's name which is very similar to God's name אֵל

_____ .

אֱלֹהֵי means "God of".

אֱלֹהֵי is part of another word meaning "our God".

Do you know this Hebrew word? _____

Lightly underline the Hebrew term "our God" each time it is read in

lines 13, 14, 20, 22, 23.

מֶתֶג A SPECIAL ACCENT MARK

When reading Hebrew, we usually accent the last syllable in the word.

The last syllable is the last letter and its vowel. Read these words.

לְעַ-מוֹ   בְּקָדְשָׁ-תוֹ   גָּדְ-לוֹ

וְהִשְׁתַּחֲ-וּוּ   קָדְ-שׁוֹ   וַיְ-הִי

If the last letter does not have a vowel, the last syllable is as follows:

מַלְ-כוּת   יִמְ-לֹךְ   הָאָ-רֶן

יַחְ-דָּו   צִ-יּוֹן   הָרַחֲ-מִים

Read the words accenting the last two letters correctly.

16

מֶתֶג is a special accent mark.

It is used when we do *not* accent the last syllable.

It tells us which other syllable to accent.

The מֶתֶג is usually placed to the left of the vowel. אֱ אֶ אָ אִי אַ

Sometimes it is placed under the letter. וּ אֹ אִ

These words are found in lines 1-12. Read and accent each word

correctly.

יְרוּשָׁלַיִם הֵיטִיבָה כְּמַעֲשֶׂיךָ מֶלֶךְ כָּמוֹךָ

אֹיְבֶיךָ וַיָּפֻצוּ וַיֹּאמֶר בִּנְסֹעַ בָּטַחְנוּ

מִירוּשָׁלַיִם מִפָּנֶיךָ מִשַּׂנְאֶיךָ וַיָּנֻסוּ

Find the words written with a מֶתֶג in lines 13-23 and write them:

_____ line 13

_____ _____ line 14

_____ _____ line 16

_____ _____ line 18

_____ _____ line 20

_____ _____ line 22

_____ _____ line 23

Read and accent each word correctly.

FINALS

Write the final Hebrew letter in these letter families.

Write the English sound below each letter.

צ _ מ _ נ _ כ כ פ פ _

__ _ _ _ _ _ _ _ _ _ _

Complete these letter families.

ב __ __ __ פ __ __ ך ש __

ת __ ע __ מ __ ן

Many words in lines 1-23 end with one of the five final letters.

Find and read each of these words without a mistake.

18

Hebrew verbs and nouns are constructed from groups of letters called

roots. Each root has a meaning that can be found in a Hebrew

dictionary. A root almost always has three letters. A root has no

vowels. One Hebrew root can be the basis for many Hebrew words.

Words built on the same root are related to each other.

מ-ל-ך is a familiar root.

Write the root here. ＿＿ ＿＿ ＿＿

מ-ל-ך is the root of the Hebrew word meaning "king".

מ-ל-ך is the root of the Hebrew word meaning "to reign" ("to rule").

Find and write each word built on the root מ-ל-ך.

Remember! To recognize a root you must recognize family letters.

＿＿＿＿＿＿＿＿＿＿ ＿＿＿＿＿＿ line   2

＿＿＿＿＿＿＿＿＿＿ ＿＿＿＿＿＿ line   4

＿＿＿＿＿＿＿＿＿＿ line   7

＿＿＿＿＿＿＿＿＿＿ line 18

19

AN IMPORTANT ROOT

ק-ד-שׁ is an important root.

Words built on this root mean "holy", "sanctify", "hallow".

Write the root here. ___ ___ ___

Find and write each word built on the root ק-ד-שׁ.

_____ line 12

_____ line 14

_____ line 20

_____ line 22

Which word appears three times? _____

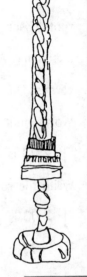

READING PRACTICE

בְּקָדְשָׁתוֹ קְדֻשָׁה קֹדֶשׁ קָדוֹשׁ

נְקַדֵשׁ קְדוּשַׁת קָדְשֶׁךָ מְקַדֵשׁ

נַקְדִישׁ מְקַדְשֵׁי שֶׁמַקְדִישִׁים וּקְדוֹשִׁים

וַ וְ וּ are prefixes meaning "and".

Find and write each word written with the prefix וַ וְ or וּ

_____ line 1

_____ line 2

_____ line 8

_____ line 9

_____ line 10

_____ line 11

_____ line 15

Complete each word. Write the missing words (lines 16-19).

לְךָ יְיָ הַגְדֻלָה וְ _____ וְ _____

וְ _____ וְ _____ כִּי כֹל בַּשָּׁמַיִם וְ _____

לְךָ יְיָ הַמַּמְלָכָה וְ _____ לְכֹל לְרֹאשׁ

Can you now read lines 1-23 fluently?

21

סֵדֶר הוֹצָאַת סֵפֶר הַתּוֹרָה

Each person called to the Torah chants two blessings. The first blessing is recited before the Torah portion is read; the second blessing is recited when that portion has been completed. The first blessing praises God for choosing the Jewish people by giving us His Torah. The second blessing praises God for the truth of the Torah. It is our connection to everlasting life.

בִּרְכוֹת הַתּוֹרָה

Each congregant honored recites the following blessings:

1 בָּרְכוּ אֶת־יְיָ הַמְבֹרָךְ.

Congregation responds:

2 בָּרוּךְ יְיָ הַמְבֹרָךְ לְעוֹלָם וָעֶד.

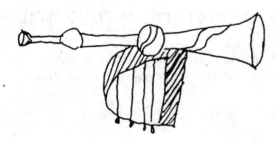

The congregant honored continues:

³ בָּרוּךְ יְיָ הַמְבֹרָךְ לְעוֹלָם וָעֶד.

⁴ בָּרוּךְ אַתָּה יְיָ, אֱלֹהֵינוּ מֶלֶךְ הָעוֹלָם,

⁵ אֲשֶׁר בָּחַר בָּנוּ מִכָּל־הָעַמִּים,

⁶ וְנָתַן לָנוּ אֶת־תּוֹרָתוֹ.

⁷ בָּרוּךְ אַתָּה יְיָ נוֹתֵן הַתּוֹרָה.

Bless the Lord who is to be blessed.
Bless the Lord who is to be blessed forever.
Blessed are You, O Lord our God, King of the universe
who chose us from among all people by giving us His
Torah. Blessed are You, O Lord, giver of the Torah.

The Torah is now read. At the conclusion of each portion, the
congregant honored recites:

⁸ בָּרוּךְ אַתָּה יְיָ, אֱלֹהֵינוּ מֶלֶךְ הָעוֹלָם,

⁹ אֲשֶׁר נָתַן לָנוּ תּוֹרַת אֱמֶת

¹⁰ וְחַיֵּי עוֹלָם נָטַע בְּתוֹכֵנוּ.

¹¹ בָּרוּךְ אַתָּה יְיָ נוֹתֵן הַתּוֹרָה.

Blessed are You, O Lord our God, King of the universe,
who in giving us a Torah of truth has planted everlasting
life within us.
Blessed are You, O Lord, giver of the Torah.

After the Torah Reading is completed, the Torah scroll is held up so that the congregation can see columns of the text. The congregation then sings:

¹²וְזֹאת הַתּוֹרָה אֲשֶׁר שָׂם מֹשֶׁה לִפְנֵי בְּנֵי
¹³יִשְׂרָאֵל, עַל פִּי יְיָ בְּיַד מֹשֶׁה.

This the Torah that Moses put before the children of Israel, at the command of the Lord, by the hand of Moses.

בִּרְכוֹת הַתּוֹרָה

Read the first בְּרָכָה

Complete the first two sentences.

Write the English meaning under each sentence.

בָּרְכוּ _____

_____

בָּרוּךְ _____

_____

Find and read the sentence which is repeated in the בְּרָכָה

Do you recognize the first two sentences from another section of the

prayer service?

These three words are included in every בְּרָכָה

בָּרוּךְ אַתָּה יְיָ "Blessed (Praised) are You, O Lord"

Write the Hebrew phrase here. _____

Find and lightly underline בָּרוּךְ אַתָּה יְיָ in each בְּרָכָה

Write the missing words.

מֶלֶךְ _____ יְיָ _____ בָּרוּךְ

Complete the final sentence of each בְּרָכָה (lines 7 and 11).

בָּרוּךְ אַתָּה יְיָ _____

בָּרוּךְ אַתָּה יְיָ _____

What did you discover?

This sentence has been translated for you.

Write the English meaning.

_____

_____

READING CHALLENGE

Can you read lines 1-4 without a mistake?

Can you read the final sentence of each בְּרָכָה fluently?

ב-ר-ך is an important root.

Words built on this root mean "bless" or "praise"

Write the root. ____ ____ ____

Read the first בְּרָכָה

Write the words in lines 1-3 built on the root ב-ר-ך

_____ _____ _____

_____ _____ _____

Which word was read twice? _____ .

Which word was read three times? _____

Write the word found in line 4 and in line 7 built on the root

ב-ר-ך _____

Read the second בְּרָכָה

Write the word found in line 8 and in line 11 built on the root

ב-ר-ך _____

28

29

בִּרְכוֹת הַתּוֹרָה

FIRST בְּרָכָה	SECOND בְּרָכָה
אֶת תּוֹרָתוֹ	וְחַיֵּי עוֹלָם
His Torah	and everlasting life
אֲשֶׁר בָּחַר בָּנוּ	אֲשֶׁר נָתַן לָנוּ
who chose us	who gave us
וְנָתַן לָנוּ	נָטַע בְּתוֹכֵנוּ
and gave us (by giving us)	planted within us
מִכָּל הָעַמִּים	תּוֹרַת אֱמֶת
from among all people	Torah of truth

Write the Key Phrases in the order they are read in each בְּרָכָה.

Write the English beneath each Hebrew phrase.

FIRST בְּרָכָה

2nd _____   1st _____

_____   _____

4th _____   3rd _____

_____   _____

SECOND בְּרָכָה

2nd _____   1st _____

_____   _____

4th _____   3rd _____

_____   _____

READING CHALLENGE

Look at each set of Key Phrases you have written.

Can you read each Key Phrase without a mistake?

Can you read the first and second phrases together?

Can you read the third and fourth phrases together?

The sentences and phrases in the בְּרָכוֹת are written in mixed-up order.

Put a number in each circle to show the correct order of the phrases within each בְּרָכָה.

First בְּרָכָה

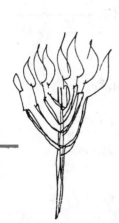

○ בָּרְכוּ אֶת־יְיָ הַמְבֹרָךְ

○ אֲשֶׁר בָּחַר בָּנוּ מִכָּל־הָעַמִּים

○ בָּרוּךְ יְיָ הַמְבֹרָךְ לְעוֹלָם וָעֶד

○ בָּרוּךְ אַתָּה יְיָ אֱלֹהֵינוּ מֶלֶךְ הָעוֹלָם

○ וְנָתַן לָנוּ אֶת־תּוֹרָתוֹ

○ בָּרוּךְ יְיָ הַמְבֹרָךְ לְעוֹלָם וָעֶד

○ בָּרוּךְ אַתָּה יְיָ נוֹתֵן הַתּוֹרָה

Second בְּרָכָה

○ בָּרוּךְ אַתָּה יְיָ

○ וְחַיֵּי עוֹלָם נָטַע בְּתוֹכֵנוּ

○ אֲשֶׁר נָתַן לָנוּ תּוֹרַת אֱמֶת

○ אֱלֹהֵינוּ מֶלֶךְ הָעוֹלָם

○ בָּרוּךְ אַתָּה יְיָ נוֹתֵן הַתּוֹרָה

Read lines 12-13.

Write the Hebrew word found in each phrase.

_____	וְזֹאת הַתּוֹרָה
Torah	This is the Torah
_____	אֲשֶׁר שָׂם מֹשֶׁה
Moses	that Moses put
_____	לִפְנֵי בְּנֵי יִשְׂרָאֵל
Israel	before the children of Israel
_____	עַל פִּי יְיָ
Lord	at the command of the Lord
_____	בְּיַד מֹשֶׁה
Moses	by the hand of Moses

Add the missing vowels.

Write each word to complete the passage.

וְזֹאת _____ אֲשֶׁר שָׂם

לִפְנֵי בְּנֵי _____ עַל פִּי _____

בְּיַד _____

This passage has been translated for you.

Write the English meaning.

_____

_____

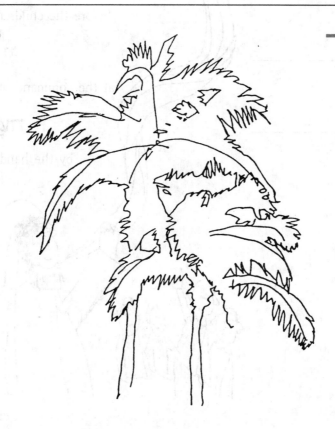

Can you unscramble the words to write the passage correctly?

לִפְנֵי עַל בְּנֵי וְזֹאת מֹשֶׁה יְיָ

יִשְׂרָאֵל בְּיַד הַתּוֹרָה מֹשֶׁה אֲשֶׁר

פִּי שָׂם

_____

_____

_____

Can you read and sing lines 1-11 easily?

Can you read and sing lines 12-13?

On Shabbat, seven people are called to the Torah. They are followed by another person (**maftir**) who chants an additional Reading from a later book of the Bible (**haftarah**). The **haftarah** consists of passages from the section of the Bible known as Prophets. First the **maftir** recites **birkhot hatorah** over the Torah portion which is read. The Torah Scroll is raised and wrapped in its adornments. There are five **haftarah** blessings. The first blessing is chanted before the **haftarah** is recited. The other four blessings are chanted after the **haftarah** has been completed.

בִּרְכוֹת הַהַפְטָרָה

BLESSING BEFORE THE HAFTARAH

1 בָּרוּךְ אַתָּה יְיָ אֱלֹהֵינוּ מֶלֶךְ הָעוֹלָם, אֲשֶׁר בָּחַר

2 בִּנְבִיאִים טוֹבִים וְרָצָה בְּדִבְרֵיהֶם הַנֶּאֱמָרִים

3 בֶּאֱמֶת. בָּרוּךְ אַתָּה יְיָ הַבּוֹחֵר בַּתּוֹרָה וּבְמשֶׁה

4 עַבְדּוֹ וּבְיִשְׂרָאֵל עַמּוֹ וּבִנְבִיאֵי הָאֱמֶת וָצֶדֶק.

Blessed are You, O Lord who has chosen the Torah, His servant Moses, His people Israel, and prophets of truth and righteousness.

THE FOUR BLESSINGS AFTER THE HAFTARAH

בָּרוּךְ אַתָּה יְיָ אֱלֹהֵינוּ מֶלֶךְ הָעוֹלָם, צוּר כָּל־ 5

הָעוֹלָמִים צַדִּיק בְּכָל־הַדּוֹרוֹת, הָאֵל הַנֶּאֱמָן 6

הָאוֹמֵר וְעוֹשֶׂה הַמְדַבֵּר וּמְקַיֵּם שֶׁכָּל־דְּבָרָיו אֱמֶת 7

וָצֶדֶק. נֶאֱמָן אַתָּה הוּא יְיָ אֱלֹהֵינוּ וְנֶאֱמָנִים 8

דְּבָרֶיךָ, וְדָבָר אֶחָד מִדְּבָרֶיךָ אָחוֹר לֹא יָשׁוּב 9

רֵיקָם, כִּי אֵל מֶלֶךְ נֶאֱמָן וְרַחֲמָן אָתָּה. בָּרוּךְ אַתָּה 10

יְיָ הָאֵל הַנֶּאֱמָן בְּכָל־דְּבָרָיו. 11

Blessed are You, O Lord, God who is faithful in fulfilling
His words.

רַחֵם עַל צִיּוֹן כִּי הִיא בֵּית חַיֵּינוּ, וְלַעֲלוּבַת נֶפֶשׁ 12

תּוֹשִׁיעַ בִּמְהֵרָה בְיָמֵינוּ. בָּרוּךְ אַתָּה יְיָ מְשַׂמֵּחַ 13

צִיּוֹן בְּבָנֶיהָ. 14

Blessed are you, O Lord who makes Zion rejoice with her
children.

¹⁵ שַׂמְּחֵנוּ יְיָ אֱלֹהֵינוּ בְּאֵלִיָּהוּ הַנָּבִיא עַבְדֶּךָ

¹⁶ וּבְמַלְכוּת בֵּית דָּוִד מְשִׁיחֶךָ. בִּמְהֵרָה יָבֹא וְיָגֵל

¹⁷ לִבֵּנוּ, עַל כִּסְאוֹ לֹא יֵשֵׁב זָר וְלֹא יִנְחֲלוּ עוֹד

¹⁸ אֲחֵרִים אֶת־כְּבוֹדוֹ. כִּי בְשֵׁם קָדְשְׁךָ נִשְׁבַּעְתָּ לּוֹ

¹⁹ שֶׁלֹּא יִכְבֶּה נֵרוֹ לְעוֹלָם וָעֶד. בָּרוּךְ אַתָּה יְיָ מָגֵן

²⁰ דָּוִד.

Bring us joy, Lord our God, through Your prophet Elijah
and the kingdom of the House of David....Praised are
You, Lord, Shield of David.

²¹ עַל הַתּוֹרָה וְעַל הָעֲבוֹדָה וְעַל הַנְּבִיאִים וְעַל יוֹם

²² הַשַּׁבָּת הַזֶּה שֶׁנָּתַתָּ לָנוּ יְיָ אֱלֹהֵינוּ לִקְדֻשָּׁה

²³ וְלִמְנוּחָה לְכָבוֹד וּלְתִפְאֶרֶת. עַל הַכֹּל יְיָ אֱלֹהֵינוּ

²⁴ אֲנַחְנוּ מוֹדִים לָךְ וּמְבָרְכִים אוֹתָךְ. יִתְבָּרַךְ שִׁמְךָ

²⁵ בְּפִי כָּל־חַי תָּמִיד לְעוֹלָם וָעֶד. בָּרוּךְ אַתָּה יְיָ

²⁶ מְקַדֵּשׁ הַשַּׁבָּת.

We thank You and praise You, Lord our God, for the
Torah, for worship, for the prophets, and for this Shabbat
day which You have given us for holiness and rest....
Praised are You, Lord who sanctifies Shabbat.

The final sentence of a בְּרָכָה begins with the words:

_____

Lightly circle these three words at the end of each

of the five בְּרָכוֹת.

Which בְּרָכוֹת also begin with the words בָּרוּךְ אַתָּה יְיָ?

Complete each of the five בְּרָכוֹת.

These sentences have been translated for you.

Tell the English meaning of each Hebrew sentence.

בָּרוּךְ אַתָּה יי הַבּוֹחֵר
_____

_____

בָּרוּךְ אַתָּה יי הָאֵל
_____

_____

בָּרוּךְ אַתָּה יי מְשַׂמֵּחַ
_____

_____

בָּרוּךְ אַתָּה יי
_____

_____

בָּרוּךְ אַתָּה יי _____

_____

_____

---- **READING CHALLENGE** ----

Can you read each concluding sentence without a mistake?

בְּרָכָה READ BEFORE THE HAFTARAH

WORD STUDY

Read the concluding sentence of the בְּרָכָה.

Write the familiar Hebrew words found in this sentence.

_____   _____   _____

ISRAEL   MOSES   TORAH

These three words are also found in the concluding sentence.

וּבִנְבִיאֵי   הָאֱמֶת   וָצֶדֶק

and prophets of   (the) truth   and righteousness

Write the six Hebrew words here:

_____   _____

_____   _____

_____   _____

Lightly underline these six words in the בְּרָכָה

FINAL ם

Find the five words ending with final ם.

Write the words in the order they are found in the בְּרָכָה.

_____ _____ _____

_____ _____

Here they are again.

Add the missing vowels.

העולם   בנביאים   טובים

בדבריהם   הנאמרים

READING CHALLENGE

Can you read the complete בְּרָכָה without a mistake?

THE FIRST בְּרָכָה

WORD STUDY

Read the concluding sentence in Hebrew and in English.

Lightly underline the phrase הָאֵל הַנֶּאֱמָן "the faithful God".

הָאֵל הַנֶּאֱמָן is read one other time in the בְּרָכָה.

Find the phrase and lightly underline it.

Write the phrase here.

44

GOD'S NAME

יְיָ   יְהֹוָה   אֲדֹנָי   אָדוֹן   אֵל   אֱלֹהִים

How is God's name pronounced when it is spelled this way? יְיָ

_____

Lightly circle God's name יְיָ each time it is found in the בְּרָכָה.

Write the two other spellings for "Adonai". _____

_____

Lightly circle אֵל in lines 6, 10 and 11.

אֱלֹהֵי means "God of".

אֱלֹהֵי is part of another word found in lines 5 and 8.

Write the word meaning "Our God" _____

Complete the words in these phrases.

בָּרוּךְ אַתָּה יְיָ אֱלֹהֵינוּ מֶלֶךְ הָעוֹלָם

נֶאֱמָן אַתָּה הוּא יְיָ אֱלֹהֵינוּ

בִּרְכוֹת הַהַפְטָרָה

א-מ-ן means "faithful".

Write the root letters. ＿＿＿ ＿＿＿ ＿＿＿

Find words with the root א-מ-ן in lines 6, 8, 10 and 11. Write them here:

＿＿＿＿＿＿＿＿＿＿ ＿＿＿＿＿＿＿＿＿＿ ＿＿＿＿＿＿＿＿＿＿

＿＿＿＿＿＿＿＿＿＿ ＿＿＿＿＿＿＿＿＿＿

ד-ב-ר means "speak" or "talk".

Write the root letters. ＿＿＿ ＿＿＿ ＿＿＿

Find words with the root ד-ב-ר in lines 7, 9 and 11. Write them here:

＿＿＿＿＿＿＿＿＿＿ ＿＿＿＿＿＿＿＿＿＿ ＿＿＿＿＿＿＿＿＿＿

＿＿＿＿＿＿＿＿＿＿ ＿＿＿＿＿＿＿＿＿＿

צ-ד-ק means "righteous" or "just".

Write the root letters. ＿＿＿ ＿＿＿ ＿＿＿

Find words with the root צ-ד-ק in lines 6 and 8. Write them here:

＿＿＿＿＿＿＿＿＿＿ ＿＿＿＿＿＿＿＿＿＿

שֶׁכָּל דְּבָרָיו אֱמֶת וָצֶדֶק

"For all His words are true and righteous".

PREFIXES

וַ וְ וּ are prefixes meaning "and".

Write the words in the בְּרָכָה written with the prefix וַ וְ or וּ
(Lines 7-10).

_____ _____ _____

_____ _____ _____

הָ הַ are prefixes meaning "the".

Write the words in the בְּרָכָה written with the prefix הַ or הָ.

_____ line 5

_____ line 6

_____

_____ line 7

_____ line 11

These words in lines 6 and 7 are written in mixed-up order.

Write them in the correct order.

הָאוֹמֵר הָאֵל הַנֶּאֱמָן וּמְקַיֵּם הַמְדַבֵּר

צַדִּיק וְעוֹשֶׂה בְּכָל הַדּוֹרוֹת הָעוֹלָמִים

_____

_____

_____

Can you now read the complete בְּרָכָה fluently?

48

WORD STUDY

Read the concluding sentence in Hebrew and in English.

Do you recognize the Hebrew word meaning "Zion"?

_____

Lightly circle it each time it is read in the בְּרָכָה.

Can you explain the significance of the word צִיּוֹן for the Jewish

people?

Complete the words in each phrase.

רחם על צִיּוֹן   משמח צִיּוֹן בבניה

Add the מֶתֶג to these vowel sounds. אִי אוּ אָ אֵ אַ אָ אִי אוּ

Seven words in this בְּרָכָה are written with the מֶתֶג

Write each of these words and complete the בְּרָכָה.

רַחֵם עַל צִיּוֹן כִּי הִיא בֵּית _____

_____

בִּמְהֵרָה _____ בָּרוּךְ אַתָּה יְיָ

_____ צִיּוֹן

Can you correctly read each word you have written?

Can you read the first seven words of the בְּרָכָה without a mistake?

Can you read the second בְּרָכָה easily?

WORD STUDY

Two well-known names from the Bible are found in this בְּרָכָה.

Read the concluding sentence in Hebrew and in English.

Do you know the English name for דָּוִד? _____

מָגֵן דָּוִד means "Shield of David".

Lightly underline מָגֵן דָּוִד in the concluding sentence.

Write the phrase. _____

בֵּית דָּוִד means "House of David".

Lightly underline בֵּית דָּוִד in line 16.

Write the phrase. _____

Do you know the English meaning of אֵלִיָּהוּ הַנָּבִיא?

_____

Lightly underline בְּאֵלִיָּהוּ הַנָּבִיא in line 15.

Write the phrase. _____

Add the vowels and מֶתֶג to complete each phrase.

מגן דוד   בית דוד   באליהו הנביא

דָּגֵשׁ A SPECIAL DOT

The דָּגֵשׁ is a special dot found in many Hebrew words.

The דָּגֵשׁ is found in the middle of a letter.

Sometimes the דָּגֵשׁ changes the sound of a letter.

Add the דָּגֵשׁ to one member in each set of family letters:

פ פ כ כ ב ב

Many times the דָּגֵשׁ does **not** affect the sound of a letter:

וּ ל מ י ד נ

Add the vowels, the מֶתֶג and דָּגֵשׁ to these words in the בְּרָכָה.

שמחנו אלהינו באליהו הנביא עבדך	line 15
בית דוד משיחך במהרה	line 16
לבנו כסאו ישב	line 17
כבודו כי נשבעת לו	line 18
שלא יכבה ברוך אתה דוד	line 19-20

READING CHALLENGE

Can you read each completed word correctly?

Can you now read the third בְּרָכָה without a mistake?

WORD STUDY

Read the concluding sentence in Hebrew and in English.

Do you recognize the Hebrew word meaning "Sabbath"? _____

Read each phrase: מְקַדֵּשׁ הַשַּׁבָּת   יוֹם הַשַּׁבָּת

Lightly underline each phrase in the בְּרָכָה.

Write each phrase. _____

_____

ק-ד-שׁ means _____

Write the words in lines 22 and 26 built on the root שׁ-ד-ק

_____

ב-ר-ך means _____

Write the words in lines 24 and 25 built on the root ך-ר-ב.

_____

KEY WORDS AND PHRASES TO READ AND UNDERSTAND

וְעַל הָעֲבוֹדָה	עַל הַתּוֹרָה
and for the worship	for the Torah
וְעַל יוֹם הַשַּׁבָּת	וְעַל הַנְּבִיאִים
and for the Sabbath day	and for the prophets

וּלְתִפְאֶרֶת	לְכָבוֹד	וְלִמְנוּחָה	לִקְדֻשָּׁה
and for glory	for honor	and for rest	for holiness

READING CHALLENGE:

Can you read each Key Word and Phrase without a mistake?

Can you read the fourth בְּרָכָה easily?

SINGING CHALLENGE:

Can you chant each בְּרָכָה correctly?

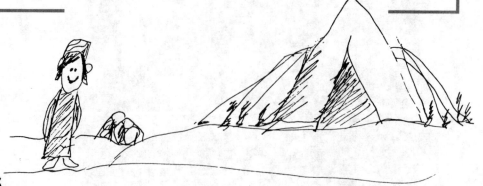

Verses from the Book of Psalms are now recited. This passage is to be recited three times daily in the discipline of Jewish prayer. It begins with the word אַשְׁרֵי. Many other passages in the Siddur are also known by their opening word.

אַשְׁרֵי

1. אַשְׁרֵי יוֹשְׁבֵי בֵיתֶךָ, עוֹד יְהַלְלוּךָ סֶּלָה.

2. אַשְׁרֵי הָעָם שֶׁכָּכָה לּוֹ, אַשְׁרֵי הָעָם שֶׁיְיָ אֱלֹהָיו.

3. תְּהִלָּה לְדָוִד

4. אֲרוֹמִמְךָ אֱלוֹהַי הַמֶּלֶךְ, וַאֲבָרְכָה שִׁמְךָ לְעוֹלָם וָעֶד.

5. בְּכָל־יוֹם אֲבָרְכֶךָּ, וַאֲהַלְלָה שִׁמְךָ לְעוֹלָם וָעֶד.

6. גָּדוֹל יְיָ וּמְהֻלָּל מְאֹד, וְלִגְדֻלָּתוֹ אֵין חֵקֶר.

7. דּוֹר לְדוֹר יְשַׁבַּח מַעֲשֶׂיךָ, וּגְבוּרֹתֶיךָ יַגִּידוּ.

8. הֲדַר כְּבוֹד הוֹדֶךָ, וְדִבְרֵי נִפְלְאֹתֶיךָ אָשִׂיחָה.

9. וֶעֱזוּז נוֹרְאֹתֶיךָ יֹאמֵרוּ, וּגְדֻלָּתְךָ אֲסַפְּרֶנָּה.

10. זֵכֶר רַב טוּבְךָ יַבִּיעוּ, וְצִדְקָתְךָ יְרַנֵּנוּ.

11. חַנּוּן וְרַחוּם יְיָ, אֶרֶךְ אַפַּיִם וּגְדָל־חָסֶד.

12. טוֹב יְיָ לַכֹּל, וְרַחֲמָיו עַל כָּל־מַעֲשָׂיו.

13. יוֹדוּךָ יְיָ כָּל־מַעֲשֶׂיךָ, וַחֲסִידֶיךָ יְבָרְכוּכָה.

14. כְּבוֹד מַלְכוּתְךָ יֹאמֵרוּ, וּגְבוּרָתְךָ יְדַבֵּרוּ.

לְהוֹדִיעַ לִבְנֵי הָאָדָם גְּבוּרֹתָיו, וּכְבוֹד הֲדַר ¹⁵
מַלְכוּתוֹ.

מַלְכוּתְךָ מַלְכוּת כָּל־עֹלָמִים, וּמֶמְשַׁלְתְּךָ ¹⁶
בְּכָל־דּוֹר וָדֹר.

סוֹמֵךְ יְיָ לְכָל־הַנֹּפְלִים, וְזוֹקֵף לְכָל־הַכְּפוּפִים. ¹⁷

עֵינֵי כֹל אֵלֶיךָ יְשַׂבֵּרוּ, וְאַתָּה נוֹתֵן לָהֶם ¹⁸
אֶת־אָכְלָם בְּעִתּוֹ.

פּוֹתֵחַ אֶת־יָדֶךָ, וּמַשְׂבִּיעַ לְכָל־חַי רָצוֹן. ¹⁹

צַדִּיק יְיָ בְּכָל־דְּרָכָיו, וְחָסִיד בְּכָל־מַעֲשָׂיו. ²⁰

קָרוֹב יְיָ לְכָל־קֹרְאָיו, לְכֹל אֲשֶׁר יִקְרָאֻהוּ בֶאֱמֶת. ²¹

רְצוֹן יְרֵאָיו יַעֲשֶׂה, וְאֶת־שַׁוְעָתָם יִשְׁמַע וְיוֹשִׁיעֵם. ²²

שׁוֹמֵר יְיָ אֶת־כָּל־אֹהֲבָיו, וְאֵת כָּל־הָרְשָׁעִים יַשְׁמִיד. ²³

תְּהִלַּת יְיָ יְדַבֶּר פִּי, וִיבָרֵךְ כָּל־בָּשָׂר שֵׁם קָדְשׁוֹ ²⁴
לְעוֹלָם וָעֶד.

וַאֲנַחְנוּ נְבָרֵךְ יָהּ, מֵעַתָּה וְעַד עוֹלָם. הַלְלוּיָהּ. ²⁵

Find and circle the title תְּהִלָּה לְדָוִד (line 3).

תְּהִלָּה לְדָוִד consists of lines 4-24.

A special pattern is found in lines 4-24.

Lightly circle the first letter in each line.

What pattern have you discovered? _____

Which letter family has not been included? _____

Complete the first word of each line.

_____ ע	_____ ח	א
_____ פ	_____ ט	ב
_____ צ	_____ י	ג
_____ ק	_____ כ	ד
_____ ר	_____ ל	ה
_____ שׁ	_____ מ	ו
_____ ת	_____ ס	ז

Can you read the first word in lines 4-24 without a mistake?

Each Key Phrase is the first half of a verse in תְּהִלָּה לְדָוִד
(lines 4-24).

I will extol You, my God, O King   אֲרוֹמִמְךָ אֱלוֹהַי הַמֶּלֶךְ

Every day will I bless You   בְּכָל־יוֹם אֲבָרְכֶךָּ

Great is the Lord and highly to be   גָּדוֹל יְיָ וּמְהֻלָּל מְאֹד
praised

One generation shall laud Your   דּוֹר לְדוֹר יְשַׁבַּח מַעֲשֶׂיךָ
works to another

The majestic glory of Your splendor   הֲדַר כְּבוֹד הוֹדֶךָ

And they shall proclaim the might of   וֶעֱזוּז נוֹרְאוֹתֶיךָ יֹאמֵרוּ
your awesome acts

They shall make known the fame of Your   זֵכֶר רַב טוּבְךָ יַבִּיעוּ
great goodness

The Lord is gracious and compassionate   חַנּוּן וְרַחוּם יְיָ

The Lord is good to all   טוֹב יְיָ לַכֹּל

All Your works shall praise You, O   יוֹדוּךָ יְיָ כָּל מַעֲשֶׂיךָ
Lord

They shall declare the glory of Your   כְּבוֹד מַלְכוּתְךָ יֹאמֵרוּ
Kingdom

To make known to the sons
of men His mighty acts
לְהוֹדִיעַ לִבְנֵי הָאָדָם גְּבוּרֹתָיו

Your kingdom is an everlasting
kingdom
מַלְכוּתְךָ מַלְכוּת כָּל־עֹלָמִים

The Lord upholds all who fall
סוֹמֵךְ יְיָ לְכָל־הַנֹּפְלִים

The eyes of all look hopefully to You
עֵינֵי כֹל אֵלֶיךָ יְשַׂבֵּרוּ

You open Your hand
פּוֹתֵחַ אֶת־יָדֶךָ

The Lord is righteous in all His ways
צַדִּיק יְיָ בְּכָל־דְּרָכָיו

The Lord is near to all who call
upon Him
קָרוֹב יְיָ לְכָל־קֹרְאָיו

He will fulfill the desire of those who
revere Him
רְצוֹן יְרֵאָיו יַעֲשֶׂה

The Lord preserves all those
who love Him
שׁוֹמֵר יְיָ אֶת־כָּל־אֹהֲבָיו

My mouth shall speak the praise
of the Lord
תְּהִלַּת יְיָ יְדַבֶּר פִּי

READING CHALLENGE

Can you read each Key Phrase without a mistake?

61

אַשְׁרֵי

Lines 1, 2 and 25 are not part of תְּהִלָּה לְדָוִד.

Lines 1 and 2 begin with the word _____

Lightly circle the word אַשְׁרֵי each time it is read.

Line 25 begins with the word _____.

What other word in line 25 begins with the prefix וֹ?

_____

The root ה-ל-ל means "praise".

Write the words read in lines 1 and 25 built on the root ה-ל-ל.

_____   _____

The root ב-ר-ך means _____ or _____.

Write the word on line 25 built on the root ב-ר-ך. _____

Find and write each word in lines 1, 2 and 25 written with a מֶתֶג.

_____   _____   _____

_____   _____

The Hebrew word סֶלָה is not translated into English.

Its meaning is unknown.

MISSING LINKS

Complete each sentence.

אַשְׁרֵי _____ _____ עוד

_____ סֶלָה

Happy are they that dwell in Your house. They will ever praise You.

אַשְׁרֵי _____ _____

_____ אַשְׁרֵי _____ שֶׁיי

_____

Happy is the people who thus fare. Happy is the people whose God is

the Lord.

וַאֲנַחְנוּ _____ יָהּ _____ וָעֵד

עוֹלָם _____

And we will bless the Lord from this time forth and forever more.

Halleluyah.

God's name is written in different ways

אֱלֹהִים אֵל אָדוֹן אֲדֹנָי יְהֹוָה יְיָ

_____

Write the three ways God's name is pronounced exactly the same.

_____ _____ _____

God's name **יְיָ** is found in line 2. Write the complete word.

_____

Write the form of God's name derived from **אֵל**. _____

אֱלֹהַי means "My God".

Complete this phrase (line 4).

אֲרוֹמִמְךָ _____ הַמֶּלֶךְ

אֱלֹהָיו means "His (the people's) God".

Complete this phrase (line 2).

_____ אַשְׁרֵי הָעָם שֶׁיְיָ

יָהּ is another form of God's name.

Add יָהּ to the list above.

Lightly circle יָהּ each time it is found in line 25.

What do you think is the English translation of הַלְלוּיָהּ? (Hint:
Remember the meaning of the root ה-ל-ל.)

_____

Complete this sentence (line 25).

וַאֲנַחְנוּ נְבָרֵךְ _____ מֵעַתָּה וְעַד עוֹלָם

_____

─── **READING CHALLENGE** ───

Can you read each Hebrew name for God without a mistake?

Can you read lines 1, 2 and 25 without a mistake?

FINALS

Write the sound for each letter. _____ כ _____ כּ

Write the word in line 2 written with both sounds.

_____

Write the sound for final ך _____

Sometimes final ך has a דָּגֵשׁ

Write the sound for final ךּ _____

Write the word with the ending ך (line 5). _____

Write the words ending ךָ which are repeated in תְּהִלָּה לְדָוִד.

lines 4 and 5 _____

lines 7 and 13 _____

lines 14 and 16 _____

Add the vowels, דָּגֵשׁ and מֶתֶג to complete each word ending ך or ךּ.

line 1	יהללוך	ביתך	
line 4	שמך	ארוממך	
line 5	שמך	אברכך	
line 7	וגבורתיך	מעשיך	
line 8	נפלאתיך	הודך	
line 9	וגדלתך	נוראותיך	
line 10	וצדקתך	טובך	
line 13	וחסידיך	מעשיך	יודוך
line 14	וגבורתך	מלכותך	
line 16	וממשלתך	מלכותך	
line 18	אליך		
line 19	ידך		

Write the words ending ךּ.

_____	_____	_____
line 4	line 11	line 17

_____	_____
line 24	line 25

67

אַשְׁרֵי

┌─────────── **READING CHALLENGE** ───────────┐

Can you read all the words ending with final **ך** without a mistake?

└───┘

┌─────────────── **MORE FINALS** ───────────────┐

Write the final form of **פ**. _____

Write the word ending with this final in line 17._____

Write the final form of **נ**. _____

Write the words ending with this final.

_____   _____   _____

       line 6   line 11   line 18

_____   _____

       line 19   line 22

Write the final form of **מ**. _____

Write the word with this final in line 2. _____

Write the Hebrew phrase meaning "Happy is the people"

_____

עוֹלָם is written in different ways.

Write each עוֹלָם word.

lines 4, 5 and 24 _____

line 16 _____

line 25 _____

Add the vowels, דָּגֵשׁ מֶתֶג and to complete these words ending with ם.

line 11	אפים	ורחום
line 15	האדם	
line 17	הכפופים	הנפלים
line 18	אכלם	להם
line 22	ויושיעם	שועתם
line 23	הרשעים	
line 24	שם	

READING CHALLENGE

Can you read each word ending with final ף ן ם without a mistake?

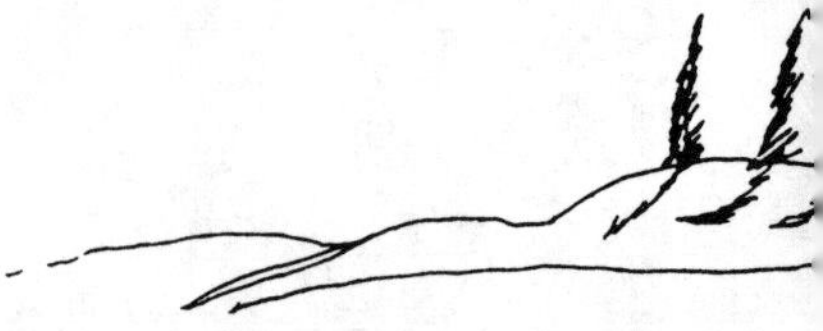

Recognize the root letters. (Hint: Remember familiy letters when searching for roots.)

ר-ח-ם means "compassion, mercy, pity".

Words built on ר-ח-ם:

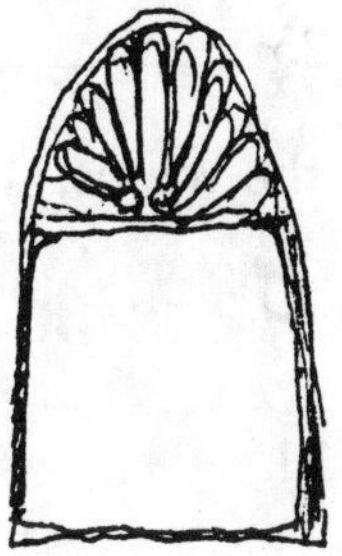

_____   _____

       line 11   line 12

ח-ס-ד means "loving kindness".

Words built on ח-ס-ד:

_____   _____   _____

      line 11   line 13   line 20

ע-ש-ה means "do, make".

Words built on ע-ש-ה:

_____   _____   _____

      line 7   line 12   line 13

_____   _____

      line 20   line 22

ה-ל-ל means _____

Words built on ה-ל-ל: _____
line 1

_____   _____   _____
line 5   line 6   line 25

ב-ר-ך means _____ or _____

Words built on ב-ר-ך:

_____   _____   _____
line 4   line 5   line 13

_____   _____
line 24   line 25

מ-ל-ך means _____ or _____.

Words built on מ-ל-ך:

_____   _____   _____
line 4   line 14   line 15

_____   _____
line 16   line 16

ק-ד-צ means _____ or _____

Words built on ק-ד-צ:

_____ _____

line 10 line 20

ר-ב-ד means _____ or _____

Words built on ר-ב-ד:

_____ _____ _____

line 8 line 14 line 24

ש-ד-ק means _____, _____ or

_____.

Word built on ש-ד-ק: _____

line 24

The Torah Scroll is returned to the Ark with special ceremony. It is carried in a procession. During the procession, a Psalm is sung. When the Torah Scroll rests in the Ark again, we sing verses from the Bible which praise the Torah and ask for God's blessings through its teachings.

סֵדֶר הַכְנָסַת סֵפֶר הַתּוֹרָה

As the Torah is returned to the Ark, the congregation rises and sings these passages in praise of God.

Reader chants while holding the Torah:

1 יְהַלְלוּ אֶת־שֵׁם יְיָ כִּי נִשְׂגָּב שְׁמוֹ לְבַדּוֹ.

Praise the Lord, for He is unique, exalted.

Congregation responds:

2 הוֹדוֹ עַל אֶרֶץ וְשָׁמָיִם וַיָּרֶם קֶרֶן לְעַמּוֹ תְּהִלָּה
3 לְכָל־חֲסִידָיו לִבְנֵי יִשְׂרָאֵל עַם קְרֹבוֹ. הַלְלוּיָהּ.

His glory encompasses heaven and earth. He exalts and extols His faithful, the people Israel who are close to Him. Halleluyah.

This psalm (Psalm 29) is chanted by the congregation during the procession which returns the Torah Scroll to the Ark.

4 מִזְמוֹר לְדָוִד

5 הָבוּ לַיָי בְּנֵי אֵלִים, הָבוּ לַיָי כָּבוֹד וָעֹז.

6 הָבוּ לַיָי כְּבוֹד שְׁמוֹ, הִשְׁתַּחֲווּ לַיָי בְּהַדְרַת

7 קֹדֶשׁ.

8 קוֹל יְיָ עַל הַמָּיִם, אֵל־הַכָּבוֹד הִרְעִים יְיָ עַל מַיִם

9 רַבִּים.

10 קוֹל יְיָ בַּכֹּחַ, קוֹל יְיָ בֶּהָדָר.

11 קוֹל יְיָ שֹׁבֵר אֲרָזִים, וַיְשַׁבֵּר יְיָ אֶת־אַרְזֵי

12 הַלְּבָנוֹן.

13 וַיַּרְקִידֵם כְּמוֹ עֵגֶל, לְבָנוֹן וְשִׂרְיוֹן כְּמוֹ

14 בֶן־רְאֵמִים.

15 קוֹל יְיָ חֹצֵב לַהֲבוֹת אֵשׁ.

16 קוֹל יְיָ יָחִיל מִדְבָּר, יָחִיל יְיָ מִדְבַּר קָדֵשׁ.

17 קוֹל יְיָ יְחוֹלֵל אַיָּלוֹת וַיֶּחֱשֹׂף יְעָרוֹת,

18 וּבְהֵיכָלוֹ כֻּלּוֹ אֹמֵר כָּבוֹד.

19 יְיָ לַמַּבּוּל יָשָׁב, וַיֵּשֶׁב יְיָ מֶלֶךְ לְעוֹלָם.

20 יְיָ עֹז לְעַמּוֹ יִתֵּן, יְיָ יְבָרֵךְ אֶת־עַמּוֹ בַשָּׁלוֹם.

Praise the Lord for His power and glory. The Lord sat enthroned at the Flood; the Lord will sit enthroned forever, bestowing strength upon His people, blessing His people with peace.

76

סֵדֶר הַכְנָסַת סֵפֶר הַתּוֹרָה

After the Torah Scroll is placed in the Ark, this passage is sung
before the curtain or doors are closed.

עֵץ חַיִּים הִיא לַמַּחֲזִיקִים בָּהּ וְתֹמְכֶיהָ מְאֻשָּׁר. 21

דְּרָכֶיהָ דַרְכֵי־נֹעַם וְכָל־נְתִיבוֹתֶיהָ שָׁלוֹם. 22

הֲשִׁיבֵנוּ יְיָ אֵלֶיךָ וְנָשׁוּבָה חַדֵּשׁ יָמֵינוּ כְּקֶדֶם. 23

It is a tree of life for those who grasp it, and all who
uphold it are blessed.
Its ways are pleasantness, and all its paths are peace.
Help us turn to You, Lord, and we shall return.
Renew our lives as in days of old.

סֵדֶר הַכְנָסַת סֵפֶר הַתּוֹרָה

Three passages are studied in this lesson.

The first: lines ＿＿ – ＿＿: the second: lines ＿＿ – ＿＿: the

third: lines ＿＿ – ＿＿

Lightly circle the title introducing the second passage (line 4).

Write the title here. ＿＿＿＿＿＿＿＿＿＿＿＿＿＿＿＿＿

God's name יְיָ appears often in מִזְמוֹר לְדָוִד.

Sometimes יְיָ is written לַיְיָ.

Circle the prexfix לַ in לַיְיָ.

Write יְיָ ＿＿＿＿＿＿＿＿＿ Write לַיְיָ. ＿＿＿＿＿＿＿＿＿

קוֹל יְיָ, "the voice of the Lord", appears seven times in the passage.

Lightly circle the phrase קוֹל יְיָ in lines 8, 10, 11, 15, 16, 17.

Lightly circle יְיָ all other times יְיָ is found in lines 5-20.

Find and circle יְיָ in line 1 and line 23.

Write God's name found in line 3. ＿＿＿＿＿＿＿＿＿

＿＿＿＿＿＿＿＿＿＿＿＿＿＿＿＿＿

Write each complete word containing each of these names.

＿＿＿＿＿＿＿＿＿＿　＿＿＿＿＿＿＿＿＿＿

What is the root of the word הַלְלוּיָהּ? ____ ____ ____

What is the meaning of this root? _____

What word in line 1 is also built on this root? _____

תְּהִלָּה is built on the same root.

Which root letter is missing in the word תְּהִלָּה? ____

Lightly circle the three words in lines 1, 2 and 3 built on the root
ה-ל-ל.

Do you know an interpretation for the word יִשְׂרָאֵל?

79

The voice of the Lord is over the waters	קוֹל יְיָ עַל הַמָּיִם
The voice of the Lord is mighty	קוֹל יְיָ בַּכֹּחַ
The voice of the Lord is full of majesty	קוֹל יְיָ בֶּהָדָר
The voice of the Lord breaks the cedars	קוֹל יְיָ שֹׁבֵר אֲרָזִים
The voice of the Lord commands rock-splitting lightning	קוֹל יְיָ חֹצֵב לַהֲבוֹת אֵשׁ
The voice of the Lord causes the desert to tremble	קוֹל יְיָ יָחִיל מִדְבָּר
The voice of the Lord strips the forest bare	קוֹל יְיָ יְחוֹלֵל אַיָּלוֹת

Complete each phrase in Hebrew and in English.

The first one has been done for you.

The voice of the Lord –

is over the waters

קוֹל יְיָ –

עַל הַמָּיִם

_____   _____

_____   _____

_____   _____

_____   _____

_____   _____

Can you read each Key Phrase without a mistake?

━━━━━━━━━━━ **VOWEL RECOGNITION** ━━━━━━━━━━━

אָ has the saying sound ＿＿＿

Complete each of the following words.

בכח	קדש	ועז	קרבו
line 10	line 7	line 5	line 3

אמר	ויחשף	חצב	שבר
line 18	line 17	line 15	line 11

נעם	ותמכיה	עז
line 22	line 21	line 20

Can you read each word without a mistake?

── LETTER RECOGNITION ──

י has the saying sound _____.

Complete each word given in the phrases written below.

Fill in the missing words.

Each missing word contains a **י**

	Line:
את שם יי _____	1
_____ הודו על ארץ	2
_____ קרן לעמו	2
לבני _____ עם קרבו	3
_____	
קול יי עַל _____	8
יי על _____ רבים	8-9
_____ כמו עגל	13
לבנון _____ כמו בן ראמים	13-14

82

16 קול יי _____ _____ מדבר

יי מדבר קדש

17 קול יי _____ _____

_____ _____ _____

19 יי למבול _____ _____ **יי**

מלך לעולם

20 יי עז לעמו _____ **יי** _____

את עמו בשלום

21 עץ _____ היא

23 חדש _____ כקדם

The letter **י** has a דָּגֵשׁ is six of the words you have written.

Write each word here.

_____ _____

_____ _____

_____ _____

Complete each word.

Fill in the missing words.

Each missing word has a **י** as part of a vowel sound.

Lines 1-3

יהללו את שם יי _____ נשגב שמו
לבדו

הודו על ארץ ושמים וירם קרן לעמו תהלה
לכל _____

_____ ישראל עם קרבו הללויה

lines 21-23

עץ _____ _____ _____

בה _____ מאשר

נעם וכל _____

שלום _____

_____ וו _____

ונשובה חדש _____ כקדם

85

סֵדֶר הַכְנָסַת סֵפֶר הַתּוֹרָה

REVIEWING FINAL LETTERS

Write the sound of each of these final letters. ____ ף ____ ן

____ ם ____ ץ ____ ך

Many words in מִזְמוֹר לְדָוִד end with the sound ים. or יָם

line 5 _____

line 8 _____ _____ _____

line 9 _____

line 11 _____

line 14 _____

Write the words in lines 2 and 21 ending ים. or יָם

_____ _____ _____

Here are more words ending with ם.

line 13 _____

line 19 _____

line 20 _____

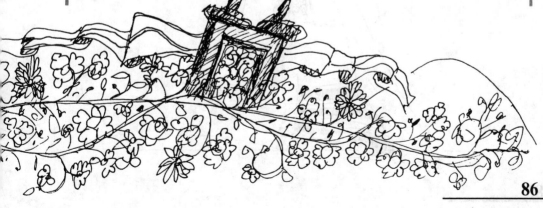

Find the words ending with these final letters ך ף ן.

line 12 _____

line 13 _____ _____

line 14 _____

line 17 _____

line 19 _____

line 20 _____ _____

Write the words in lines 2 and 21 ending with ץ.

_____ _____

Can you read each word you have written without a mistake?

סֵדֶר הַכְנָסַת סֵפֶר הַתּוֹרָה

Here are some letter patterns that are repeated in מִזְמוֹר לְדָוִד.
Recognize and write each word.

כבוד _____   _____

line 5   line 6

_____   _____

line 8   line 18

קדש _____   _____

line 7   line 16

הדר _____   _____

line 6   line 10

ארזי _____   _____

line 11   line 11

שבר _____   _____

line 11   line 11

לבנון _____   _____

line 12   line 13

ישב _____   _____

line 19   line 19

Can you find other letter patterns in מִזְמוֹר לְדָוִד?

(Hint: Look at lines 8, 13, 16 and 20.)

Can you read each word you have written without a mistake?

Can you now read מִזְמוֹר לְדָוִד fluently?

SINGING CHALLENGE

Can you sing the three prayer passages easily?

קַדִּישׁ שָׁלֵם ("Complete Kaddish") is also known as the **Reader's Kaddish**. There are several forms of **Kaddish** in the prayer service. They separate sections of the service. **Hatzi Kaddish** consists of lines 1-8. The **Mourner's Kaddish** leaves out lines 9 and 10. The **Kaddish**, in all forms, is an act of praising God in public. It is recited only in the presence of at least a minyan of ten, the minimum number required to hold a public service. The **Kaddish** is written in Aramaic (except for lines 13-14).

קַדִּישׁ שָׁלֵם

Reader

1. יִתְגַּדַּל וְיִתְקַדַּשׁ שְׁמֵהּ רַבָּא בְּעָלְמָא דִּי בְרָא כִרְעוּתֵהּ,

2. וְיַמְלִיךְ מַלְכוּתֵהּ בְּחַיֵּיכוֹן וּבְיוֹמֵיכוֹן וּבְחַיֵּי דְכָל־

3. בֵּית יִשְׂרָאֵל, בַּעֲגָלָא וּבִזְמַן קָרִיב, וְאִמְרוּ אָמֵן.

Congregation and Reader

4. יְהֵא שְׁמֵהּ רַבָּא מְבָרַךְ לְעָלַם וּלְעָלְמֵי עָלְמַיָּא.

5 יִתְבָּרַךְ וְיִשְׁתַּבַּח וְיִתְפָּאַר וְיִתְרֹמַם וְיִתְנַשֵּׂא

6 וְיִתְהַדָּר וְיִתְעַלֶּה וְיִתְהַלָּל שְׁמֵהּ דְּקֻדְשָׁא, בְּרִיךְ

7 הוּא, לְעֵלָּא מִן כָּל־בִּרְכָתָא וְשִׁירָתָה, תֻּשְׁבְּחָתָא

8 וְנֶחֱמָתָא דַּאֲמִירָן בְּעָלְמָא, וְאִמְרוּ אָמֵן.

9 תִּתְקַבַּל צְלוֹתְהוֹן וּבָעוּתְהוֹן דְּכָל־יִשְׂרָאֵל קֳדָם

10 אֲבוּהוֹן דִּי בִשְׁמַיָּא, וְאִמְרוּ אָמֵן.

11 יְהֵא שְׁלָמָא רַבָּא מִן שְׁמַיָּא וְחַיִּים עָלֵינוּ וְעַל כָּל־

12 יִשְׂרָאֵל, וְאִמְרוּ אָמֵן.

13 עֹשֶׂה שָׁלוֹם בִּמְרוֹמָיו הוּא יַעֲשֶׂה שָׁלוֹם עָלֵינוּ

14 וְעַל כָּל־יִשְׂרָאֵל, וְאִמְרוּ אָמֵן.

May He who makes peace in the heavens make peace for
us and for all Israel, and let us say: Amen.

Write the name of the prayer passage. _____

Do you recognize the root letters in the word קַדִּישׁ? ___ ___ ___

Write the English translations of the root. _____,

_____ , _____

Read line 1 in the passage.

Fill in the missing word. Lightly circle the root.

יִתְגַּדַּל _____ שְׁמֵהּ רַבָּא

"magnified and sanctified be His great name"

Another word built on this root is found in line 6: _____

Lightly circle the word תִּתְקַבַּל in line 9.

Write the word here: _____

This sentence asks God to accept the prayers offered by "all of

Israel": כָּל יִשְׂרָאֵל

Write the phrase. _____

Complete the words in lines 9 and 10.

תִּתְקַבַּל צְלוֹתְהוֹן וּבָעוּתְהוֹן דְּכָל־יִשְׂרָאֵל קֳדָם

אֲבוּהוֹן דִּי בִשְׁמַיָּא וְאִמְרוּ אָמֵן

May the prayers and pleas of the whole House of Israel be accepted by
our Father in Heaven. And let us say: Amen.

קַדִּיש שָׁלֵם asks God to establish peace:

יַעֲשֶׂה שָׁלוֹם   עֹשֶׂה שָׁלוֹם

Complete these two phrases: שלום _____

שלום _____

Read line 13.

Lightly circle both phrases.

וְאִמְרוּ אָמֵן "and let us say: Amen"

Write the phrase here. _____

Do you know the meaning of the word אָמֵן? _____

קַדִּיש שָׁלֵם is found five times in וְאִמְרוּ אָמֵן.

Lightly circle וְאִמְרוּ אָמֵן each time it is read.

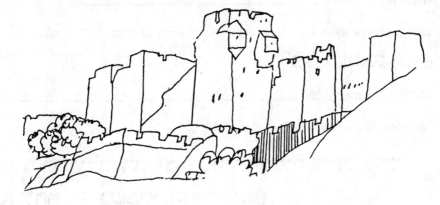

Complete the final sentence in קַדִּישׁ שָׁלֵם.

במרומיו הוא _____ _____

עלינו ועל _____ _____

ואמרו _____ _____

_____

This sentence has been translated for you.

Write the English meaning here.

_____

_____

_____

── READING CHALLENGE ──

Can you read the concluding sentence in קַדִּישׁ שָׁלֵם without a mistake?

── SINGING CHALLENGE ──

Can you now sing the sentence?

וְיִתְקַדַּשׁ

and sanctified

יִתְגַּדַּל

magnified

וְיִתְפָּאַר

and glorified

וְיִשְׁתַּבַּח

and praised

יִתְבָּרַךְ

blessed

וְיִתְהַדָּר

and honored

וְיִתְנַשֵּׂא

and extolled

וְיִתְרֹמֵם

and exalted

וְיִתְהַלָּל

and lauded

וְיִתְעַלֶּה

and adored

── ANALYZING THE KEY WORDS ──

Seven Key Words have the same pattern.

Lightly circle the common letters in each of the words above.

Write the letters here. ⎯⎯ ⎯⎯ ⎯⎯

Two of the Key Words have the common letters **ית**

Write each word. ⎯⎯⎯⎯⎯⎯⎯⎯⎯⎯ ⎯⎯⎯⎯⎯⎯⎯⎯⎯⎯

Find and lightly circle these two words in lines 1 and 5.

Write the two Key Words that begin line 1.

ית _____ וית _____

Write the two Key Words that begin line 5.

ית _____ ויש _____

Write the words in the order they appear in the passage.

ית _____
וית _____
ית _____
ויש _____
וית _____
וית _____
וית _____
וית _____
וית _____
וית _____

קַדִּישׁ שָׁלֵם

Can you read each KEY WORD without a mistake?

The words below begin on line 5.

Complete each word.

יתברך וישתבח ויתפאר ויתרמם ויתנשא
ויתהדר ויתעלה ויתהלל שמה דקדשא בריך
הוא

Can you now read these words fluently?

Answer the following.

Begin on the RIGHT!

line 2: words ending כּוֹן _____ _____

lines 7-8: words ending תָּא _____

_____ _____

lines 9-10: words ending הוֹן _____

_____ _____

line 11: words ending אָ _____ _____

_____

READING CHALLENGE

Can you read each set of words easily?

Can you now read lines 1-3, 5-8, 9-10, and 11-12 without a mistake?

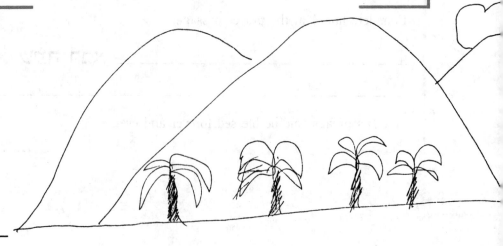

קַדִּישׁ שָׁלֵם

ב-ר-ך means _____, _____

Write the family members: ב ____ ך ____ ____

Write each word built on ב-ר-ך.

line 4 _____

line 5 _____

lines 6-7 _____ _____

ע-ל-ם means "world" or "forever".

Write the root letters. ____ ____ ____

Write the family member. ם ____

Write the words built on ע-ל-ם. Begin on the RIGHT!

line 1 _____

line 4 _____ _____

line 8 _____

Which word was repeated? _____

Complete line 4 in the prayer passage.

_____ יהא שמה רבא

_____

May His great name be blessed forever and ever.

Can you read the words built on the roots ב-ר-ך and ע-ל-ם

without a mistake?

Can you now read line 4 fluently?

━━ **MEMORY CHALLENGE** ━━

Can you sing the congregational response by heart?

The response is written in mixed-up order.

Can you write it correctly?

וּלְעָלְמֵי יְהֵא מְבָרַך לְעָלַם שְׁמֵהּ עָלְמַיָּא רַבָּא

_____

_____

_____

━━ **READING CHALLENGE** ━━

Can you read the complete passage without a mistake?

101
קַדִּישׁ שָׁלֵם

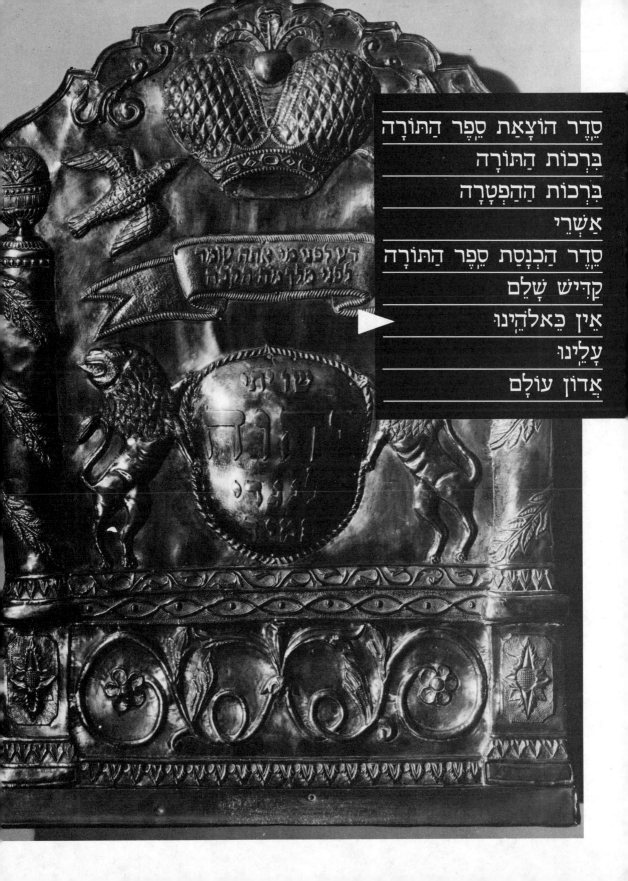

Jews have been singing this praise of God for more than a thousand years. Originally, the song began with the question in lines 3 and 4. Later the order was changed so that the first letters of lines 1-2, 3-4, and 5-6 spell the word **Amen**. The first words of lines 7-8 and 9-10 are the first words of every Hebrew blessing. In the final sentence, we link ourselves to our ancestors, recalling the offerings brought in ancient times.

אֵין כֵּאלֹהֵינוּ

אֵין כַּאדוֹנֵינוּ,	¹ אֵין כֵּאלֹהֵינוּ,
אֵין כְּמוֹשִׁיעֵנוּ.	² אֵין כְּמַלְכֵּנוּ,
מִי כַאדוֹנֵינוּ,	³ מִי כֵאלֹהֵינוּ,
מִי כְמוֹשִׁיעֵנוּ.	⁴ מִי כְמַלְכֵּנוּ,
נוֹדֶה לַאדוֹנֵינוּ,	⁵ נוֹדֶה לֵאלֹהֵינוּ,
נוֹדֶה לְמוֹשִׁיעֵנוּ.	⁶ נוֹדֶה לְמַלְכֵּנוּ,
בָּרוּךְ אֲדוֹנֵינוּ,	⁷ בָּרוּךְ אֱלֹהֵינוּ,
בָּרוּךְ מוֹשִׁיעֵנוּ.	⁸ בָּרוּךְ מַלְכֵּנוּ,
אַתָּה הוּא אֲדוֹנֵינוּ,	⁹ אַתָּה הוּא אֱלֹהֵינוּ,
אַתָּה הוּא מוֹשִׁיעֵנוּ.	¹⁰ אַתָּה הוּא מַלְכֵּנוּ,

¹¹ אַתָּה הוּא שֶׁהִקְטִירוּ אֲבוֹתֵינוּ לְפָנֶיךָ אֶת־קְטֹרֶת

¹² הַסַּמִּים.

How many sets of lines are there in the prayer passage? _____

Mark off each set of lines with this bracket].

How many phrases are found in each set? _____

These words introduce the phrases:

אֵין מִי נוֹדֶה בָּרוּךְ אַתָּה הוּא

Lightly circle these terms each time they are found in the passage.

Write these introductory words in the correct space.

line 1-2 _____   lines 5-6 _____

line 3-4 _____   lines 7-8 _____

lines 9-10 _____

Write the phrase that introduces the concluding sentence (line 11).

_____

Complete the concluding sentence.

אבותינו _____ הוּא _____

_____ _____ אֵת _____

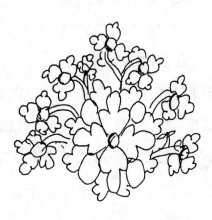

Can you read the concluding sentence without a mistake?

── MEMORY CHALLENGE ──

The words introducing the phrases in lines 1-10 are written in

mixed-up order.

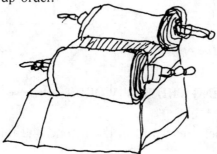

אַתָּה הוּא

אֵין

בָּרוּךְ

נוֹדֶה

מִי

Can you write them in the order they are found in the passage?

lines 1-2 _____

lines 3-4 _____

lines 5-6 _____

lines 7-8 _____

lines 9-10 _____

KEY WORDS TO READ AND UNDERSTAND

מוֹשִׁיעַ	מֶלֶךְ	אָדוֹן	אֱלֹהֵי
Savior	King	Master of	God of

אֲדוֹנֵינוּ		אֱלֹהֵינוּ
our_____		our_____

מוֹשִׁיעֵנוּ		מַלְכֵּנוּ
our_____		our_____

ANALYZING THE KEY WORDS

Write the suffix added to each Key Word in the second and third

rows. _____

What is the meaning of that suffix? _____

Complete the English meaning of each Key Word.

Read lines 1-6 in the passage.

Lightly circle the **prefix** attached to each Key Word.

Write each Key Word with its prefix and its suffix.

lines 1-2 _____ אֵין   _____ אֵין

_____ אֵין   _____ אֵין

lines 3-4 _____ מִי   _____ מִי

_____ מִי   _____ מִי

lines 5-6 _____ נוֹדֶה   _____ נוֹדֶה

_____ נוֹדֶה   _____ נוֹדֶה

Read lines 7-10 in the passage.

Write each Key Word with its suffix.

lines 7-8 _____ בָּרוּךְ   _____ בָּרוּךְ

_____ בָּרוּךְ   _____ בָּרוּךְ

lines 9-10 _____ אַתָּה הוּא   _____ אַתָּה הוּא

_____ אַתָּה הוּא   _____ אַתָּה הוּא

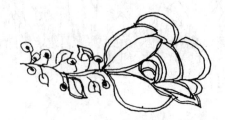

אֵין כֵּאלֹהֵינוּ

Can you read each set of words without a mistake?

Can you now read אֵין כֵּאלֹהֵינוּ fluently?

Can you sing the complete passage easily?

Each set of lines is placed out of order.

Put a number in each circle to show the correct order of the

sentences.

○ אֵין כֵּאלֹהֵינוּ, אֵין כַּאדוֹנֵינוּ,
אֵין כְּמַלְכֵּנוּ, אֵין כְּמוֹשִׁיעֵנוּ.

○ בָּרוּךְ אֱלֹהֵינוּ, בָּרוּךְ אֲדוֹנֵינוּ,
בָּרוּךְ מַלְכֵּנוּ, בָּרוּךְ מוֹשִׁיעֵינוּ.

○ מִי כֵאלֹהֵינוּ, מִי כַאדוֹנֵינוּ,
מִי כְמַלְכֵּנוּ, מִי כְמוֹשִׁיעֵנוּ.

○ אַתָּה הוּא אֱלֹהֵינוּ, אַתָּה הוּא אֲדוֹנֵינוּ,
אַתָּה הוּא מַלְכֵּנוּ, אַתָּה הוּא מוֹשִׁיעֵנוּ.

○ נוֹדֶה לֵאלֹהֵינוּ, נוֹדֶה לַאדוֹנֵינוּ,
נוֹדֶה לְמַלְכֵּנוּ, נוֹדֶה לְמוֹשִׁיעֵנוּ.

○ אַתָּה הוּא שֶׁהִקְטִירוּ אֲבוֹתֵינוּ לְפָנֶיךָ אֶת־קְטֹרֶת
הַסַּמִּים.

The first passage of עָלֵינוּ affirms the uniqueness of the Jewish people and our allegiance to God alone, the Creator "who is in the heavens above and on earth below. There is no other." The second passage stresses the necessity for all people on earth to maintain ultimate allegiance only to God. Jews reciting עָלֵינוּ at the end of each service daily envision and pray for the universal recognition of God by all people united in harmony.

עָלֵינוּ

1 עָלֵינוּ לְשַׁבֵּחַ לַאֲדוֹן הַכֹּל, לָתֵת גְּדֻלָּה לְיוֹצֵר

2 בְּרֵאשִׁית, שֶׁלֹּא עָשָׂנוּ כְּגוֹיֵי הָאֲרָצוֹת וְלֹא שָׂמָנוּ

3 כְּמִשְׁפְּחוֹת הָאֲדָמָה, שֶׁלֹּא שָׂם חֶלְקֵנוּ כָּהֶם

4 וְגֹרָלֵנוּ כְּכָל־הֲמוֹנָם.

5 וַאֲנַחְנוּ כּוֹרְעִים וּמִשְׁתַּחֲוִים וּמוֹדִים לִפְנֵי מֶלֶךְ

6 מַלְכֵי הַמְּלָכִים הַקָּדוֹשׁ בָּרוּךְ הוּא, שֶׁהוּא נוֹטֶה

7 שָׁמַיִם וְיוֹסֵד אָרֶץ, וּמוֹשַׁב יְקָרוֹ בַּשָּׁמַיִם מִמַּעַל

8 וּשְׁכִינַת עֻזּוֹ בְּגָבְהֵי מְרוֹמִים. הוּא אֱלֹהֵינוּ, אֵין

9 עוֹד. אֱמֶת מַלְכֵּנוּ, אֶפֶס זוּלָתוֹ, כַּכָּתוּב בְּתוֹרָתוֹ:

10 וְיָדַעְתָּ הַיּוֹם וַהֲשֵׁבֹתָ אֶל לְבָבֶךָ כִּי יְיָ הוּא

11 הָאֱלֹהִים בַּשָּׁמַיִם מִמַּעַל וְעַל הָאָרֶץ מִתָּחַת, אֵין

12 עוֹד.

עַל כֵּן נְקַוֶּה לְּךָ יְיָ אֱלֹהֵינוּ לִרְאוֹת מְהֵרָה 13

בְּתִפְאֶרֶת עֻזֶּךָ, לְהַעֲבִיר גִּלּוּלִים מִן הָאָרֶץ 14

וְהָאֱלִילִים כָּרוֹת יִכָּרֵתוּן, לְתַקֵּן עוֹלָם בְּמַלְכוּת 15

שַׁדַּי וְכָל־בְּנֵי בָשָׂר יִקְרְאוּ בִשְׁמֶךָ, לְהַפְנוֹת אֵלֶיךָ 16

כָּל־רִשְׁעֵי אָרֶץ. יַכִּירוּ וְיֵדְעוּ כָּל־יוֹשְׁבֵי תֵבֵל כִּי 17

לְךָ תִכְרַע כָּל־בֶּרֶךְ תִּשָּׁבַע כָּל־לָשׁוֹן. לְפָנֶיךָ יְיָ 18

אֱלֹהֵינוּ יִכְרְעוּ וְיִפּוֹלוּ. וְלִכְבוֹד שִׁמְךָ יְקָר יִתֵּנוּ, 19

וִיקַבְּלוּ כֻלָּם אֶת־עוֹל מַלְכוּתֶךָ וְתִמְלוֹךְ עֲלֵיהֶם 20

מְהֵרָה לְעוֹלָם וָעֶד, כִּי הַמַּלְכוּת שֶׁלְּךָ הִיא 21

וּלְעוֹלְמֵי עַד תִּמְלוֹךְ בְּכָבוֹד, כַּכָּתוּב בְּתוֹרָתֶךָ: יְיָ 22

יִמְלֹךְ לְעוֹלָם וָעֶד. וְנֶאֱמַר: וְהָיָה יְיָ לְמֶלֶךְ עַל כָּל־ 23

הָאָרֶץ בַּיּוֹם הַהוּא יִהְיֶה יְיָ אֶחָד וּשְׁמוֹ אֶחָד. 24

עָלֵינוּ· calls upon us to praise "the Lord of all" אֲדוֹן הַכֹּל

Read lines 1 and 3 in the passage.

Complete the phrases.

הכל _____ עלינו

It is for us to praise the Lord of all

כהם _____ שלא שם

He has not made our destiny as theirs (other people)

עָלֵינוּ· calls upon us to praise God, the "King of kings"

מֶלֶךְ מַלְכֵי הַמְּלָכִים

Read lines 5 and 6.

Complete the phrases.

ומודים _____ ואנחנו

_____ לפני

הוא _____ הקדוש

We bend the knee, worship and give thanks to the King of kings, the Holy One blessed be He

עָלֵינוּ· calls upon us to recognize God as the Lord in the "heavens above and on the earth beneath"

בַּשָׁמַיִם מִמַּעַל וְעַל הָאָרֶץ מִתָּחַת

Read lines 10-12.

Complete the phrase.

יי הוא האלהים _____

_____ אין עוד _____

The Lord is God in the heavens above and on the earth beneath; there

is none else.

עָלֵינוּ calls upon all to recognize that "God is One and His name is One

יִיָ אֶחָד וּשְׁמוֹ אֶחָד

Read lines 22-24.

Complete the sentences.

לעולם _____ יי :_____ ככתוב

ועד.

על כל _____ יי _____ :ונאמר

_____ ביום ההוא יהיה _____

_____

As it is written in Your Torah: The Lord shall reign forever and ever.

And it has been said: The Lord shall be King over all the earth. On

that day the Lord shall be One and His name One.

===== READING CHALLENGE =====

Can you read each completed phrase and sentence without a mistake?

===== KEY PHRASES TO READ AND UNDERSTAND =====

וְיוֹסֵד אָרֶץ   שֶׁהוּא נוֹטֶה שָׁמַיִם

and laid the foundations of the earth   He stretched out the heavens

וּשְׁכִינַת עֻזּוֹ   בַּשָּׁמַיִם מִמַּעַל   וּמוֹשַׁב יְקָרוֹ

His might is manifest   in the heavens above   His glorious abode

בְּגָבְהֵי מְרוֹמִים

in the loftiest heights

אֶפֶס זוּלָתוֹ   אֱמֶת מַלְכֵּנוּ

there is nothing beside Him   in truth He is our King

Complete each Hebrew phrase.

Write the English beneath each phrase.

1. שהוא _____ שמים   2. _____ ארץ

_____   _____

_____   _____

3. _____ יקרו   4. ממעל _____

_____   _____

_____   _____

5. _____ עזו   6. _____ מרומים

_____   _____

_____   _____

7. _____ מלכנו   8. _____ זולתו

_____   _____

_____   _____

--- READING CHALLENGE ---

Can you read each Key Phrase without a mistake?

Can you now read lines 5-9 fluently?

God's name is written in different ways.

אֱלֹהִים   אֵל   אָדוֹן   אֲדֹנָי   יְהֹוָה   יְיָ

יָהּ _____

Write the three ways to spell "Adonai": _____

_____ _____

שַׁדַּי is new to you.

שַׁדַּי means "the Almighty".

Read lines 15-16 in עָלֵינוּ.

Lightly circle שַׁדַּי.

Complete the phrase.

לתקן _____ שדי

We hope for the day when God will perfect the world by His almighty kingship.

Add שַׁדַּי to the list above.

אֱלֹהֵינוּ means _____.

Complete each phrase.

lines 13-14   _____ על כן נקוה לך יי

לראות מהרה בתפארת עזך

lines 18-19   לפניך יי _____ יכרעו ויפולו

Can you read each of God's names easily?

Can you read the phrases you have completed without any mistakes?

────── דָּגֵשׁ REVIEW ──────

Many times the דָּגֵשׁ does **not** change the sound of a letter.

Find and write these words in lines 13-24.

_____

_____

_____

_____

_____

────── CHALLENGE ──────

Find and read other words in the passage that have a silent דָּגֵשׁ.

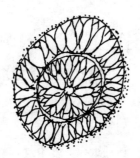

AN IMPORTANT ROOT

מ-ל-ך means _____ _____

Write each word built on the root מ-ל-ך

_____ _____ _____ lines 5-6

_____ line 9

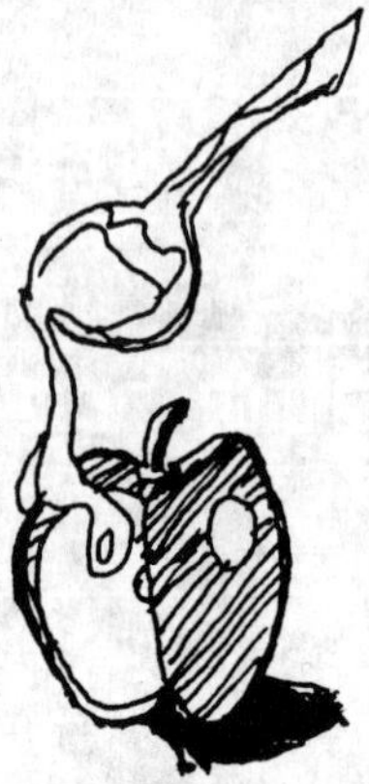

_____ line 15

_____ _____ line 20

_____ line 21

_____ line 22

_____ line 23

READING CHALLENGE

Can you read lines 5-6 and 22-24 fluently?

Can you read the entire prayer passage without a mistake?

SINGING CHALLENGE

Can you now sing lines 5-6 and 20-24?

Can you sing these lines by heart?

אֲדוֹן עוֹלָם is one of the most beautiful poems in our prayerbook. It was probably written in medieval times. The author is not known. The poem sings of God alone as eternal, without beginning and without end. We praise God as Redeemer and Guardian, and we express our deep trust in God in every situation, throughout our lives. אֲדוֹן עוֹלָם is also included in the daily early morning service and in prayers before going to sleep.

אֲדוֹן עוֹלָם

1 אֲדוֹן עוֹלָם אֲשֶׁר מָלַךְ	בְּטֶרֶם כָּל־יְצִיר נִבְרָא.
2 לְעֵת נַעֲשָׂה בְחֶפְצוֹ כֹּל	אֲזַי מֶלֶךְ שְׁמוֹ נִקְרָא.
3 וְאַחֲרֵי כִּכְלוֹת הַכֹּל	לְבַדּוֹ יִמְלוֹךְ נוֹרָא.
4 וְהוּא הָיָה וְהוּא הֹוֶה	וְהוּא יִהְיֶה בְּתִפְאָרָה.
5 וְהוּא אֶחָד וְאֵין שֵׁנִי	לְהַמְשִׁיל לוֹ לְהַחְבִּירָה.
6 בְּלִי רֵאשִׁית בְּלִי תַכְלִית	וְלוֹ הָעֹז וְהַמִּשְׂרָה.
7 וְהוּא אֵלִי וְחַי גּוֹאֲלִי	וְצוּר חֶבְלִי בְּעֵת צָרָה.
8 וְהוּא נִסִּי וּמָנוֹס לִי	מְנָת כּוֹסִי בְּיוֹם אֶקְרָא.
9 בְּיָדוֹ אַפְקִיד רוּחִי	בְּעֵת אִישַׁן וְאָעִירָה.
10 וְעִם רוּחִי גְּוִיָּתִי	יְיָ לִי וְלֹא אִירָא.

אֲדוֹן עוֹלָם is a poem written in praise of God.

Write the final word read in each line.

line 1 _____   line 6 _____

2 _____   7 _____

3 _____   8 _____

4 _____   9 _____

5 _____   10 _____

What pattern did you discover?

The second half of each line is written in mixed-up order.

Read the passage. Write each half correctly.

1 נִבְרָא כָּל בְּטֶרֶם יְצִיר   4 יִהְיֶה בְּתִפְאָרָה וְהוּא

_____   _____

_____   _____

2 מֶלֶךְ נִקְרָא אֲזַי שְׁמוֹ   5 לוֹ לְהַמְשִׁיל לְהַחְבִּירָה

_____   _____

_____   _____

3 יִמְלוֹךְ נוֹרָא לְבַדּוֹ   6 הָעֹז וְהַמִּשְׂרָה וְלוֹ

_____   _____

_____   _____

7 צָרָה בְּעֵת חֶבְלִי וְצוּר 9 בְּעֵת וְאָעִירָה אִישַׁן

_____ _____

8 כּוֹסִי אֶקְרָא בְּיוֹם מְנָת 10 אִירָא יְיָ וְלֹא לִי

_____ _____

MORE PATTERNS

Lines 4, 5, 7 and 8 begin with the same Hebrew word.

_____

Lightly circle the word each time it is read in these lines.

How many times did you find וְהוּא? _____

Complete each phrase:

וְהוּא יִהְיֶה בְּתִפְאָרָה	וְהוּא הָיָה וְהוּא הֹוֶה
לְהַמְשִׁיל לוֹ לְהַחְבִּירָה	וְהוּא אֶחָד וְאֵין שֵׁנִי
וְצוּר חֶבְלִי בְּעֵת צָרָה	וְהוּא אֵלִי וְחַי גּוֹאֲלִי
מְנָת כּוֹסִי בְּיוֹם אֶקְרָא	וְהוּא נִסִּי וּמָנוֹס לִי

123
אֲדוֹן עוֹלָם

Can you read each line without a mistake?

────── דָּגֵשׁ **REVIEW** ──────

Each line in אֲדוֹן עוֹלָם has words written with a דָּגֵשׁ.

Write each word written with a דָּגֵשׁ that does **not** change the sound of the letter.

_____   _____   _____

line 3   line 6   line 7

_____   _____

line 8   line 10

Complete each phrase with the words you have written. Add the missing vowels.

_____ ימלוך נורא

ולו העז _____

והוא אלי וחי _____

והוא _____ ומנוס לי

_____ ועם רוחי

When the **י** is a letter it has the saying sound _____.

Often the **י** is part of a vowel sound.

Write the sound of each vowel.

וִי וֹ ִי. ִי ֵ ִי ֶ יָו ִי ָ ִי ֵ ִי ַ

____ ____ ____ ____ ____ ____ ____ ____

Write each word that has **י** as a letter.

_____	_____
line 1	line 8
_____	_____
line 3	line 9
_____ _____	_____
line 4 line 4	line 10

אֲדוֹן עוֹלָם

Write each word that has **י** as part of a vowel sound.

Line:

_____ 1

_____ 2

_____ 3

_____ _____ _____ 5

_____

_____ _____ _____ 6

_____

_____ _____ _____ 7

_____

_____ _____ _____ 8

_____ _____ _____ 9

_____

_____ _____ _____ 10

_____

Write the two words found in both lists.

_____ _____

How do you pronounce **יָי** _____

אֲדוֹן עוֹלָם

Can you read each set of words easily?

Can you now read the complete prayer passage fluently?

Can you sing אֲדוֹן עוֹלָם?

Do you know another melody?

CONCLUSION

You are now familiar with a basic and very important part of our prayerbook. You can take part in the synagogue service with understanding. You have not only become more familiar with the Hebrew language, you have also learned some of the basic beliefs and ideas of the Jewish tradition. And anyone who has this knowledge should feel proud.

It has been said that the Bible contains the words of God addressed to human beings. The prayerbook contains the words which we, with all of our limitations, address to God. Prayer is essential to Jewish tradition. When you participate in prayer services, you make us stronger as a Jewish community whose basic institution is the synagogue and whose basic activity is prayer.